In My Backyard

I SEE A LADYBUG

By Alex Appleby

Gareth Stevens
Publishing

Please visit our website, www.garethstevens.com. For a free color catalog of all our high-quality books, call toll free 1-800-542-2595 or fax 1-877-542-2596.

Library of Congress Cataloging-in-Publication Data

Appleby, Alex.
 I see a ladybug / Alex Appleby.
    p. cm. — (In my backyard)
 Includes index.
 ISBN 978-1-4339-8556-0 (paperback)
 ISBN 978-1-4339-8557-7 (6-pack)
 ISBN 978-1-4339-8555-3 (library binding)
 1. Ladybugs—Juvenile literature. I. Title.
 QL596.C65A66 2013
 595.76'9—dc23

                                    2012020693

First Edition

Published in 2013 by
Gareth Stevens Publishing
111 East 14th Street, Suite 349
New York, NY 10003

Editor: Ryan Nagelhout
Designer: Katelyn Londino

Photo credits: Cover, p. 1 Vaclav Volrab/Shutterstock.com; p. 5 Ian Grainger/Shutterstock.com; pp. 7, 17, 21, 23 iStockphoto/Thinkstock.com; p. 9 Margo Sokolovskaya/Shutterstock.com; p. 11 Rudchenko Liliia/Shutterstock.com; pp. 13, 24 (wings) Symbiot/Shutterstock.com; p. 15 Hemera/Thinkstock.com; pp. 19, 24 (pests) forestpath/ Shutterstock.com; p. 24 (trees) Comstock/Thinkstock.com.

Printed in the United States of America

CPSIA compliance information: Batch #CW13GS: For further information contact Gareth Stevens, New York, New York at 1-800-542-2595.

Contents

A ladybug is small
and round.

5

It is often red
with black dots.

7

Its colors keep it safe.
Animals know
it tastes bad!

It can fly!

Its wings are hidden on its back.

13

Its wings are very fast.
They beat 85 times
a second!

It likes to eat bugs.
This is its food.

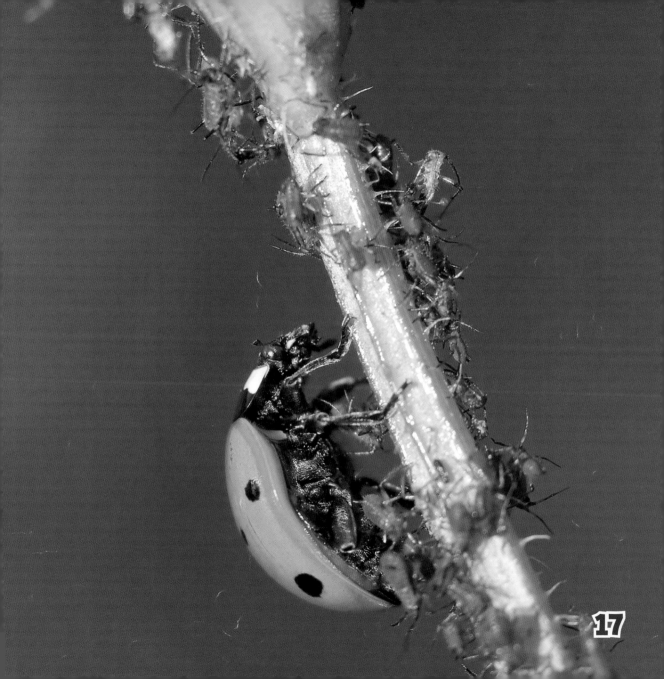

17

Farmers love ladybugs!
They eat pests
that hurt plants.

19

They hide in groups when it gets cold. This is called hibernation.

21

They stay in dead trees
or under rocks.
They come back out
in the spring!

23

Words to Know

pests

trees

wings

Index